# NOTHING
## ABOUT THIS IS
# EASY
## AND HERE IS
# WHY

**Life Through the Eyes of a Woman
on the Autism Spectrum**

*Best Wishes & Happiness
—Mari Stein*

## MARI STEIN

# Disclaimer

Names are fictional or have been changed
to protect the innocent and the guilty.

Jackson Pollock painting the ASD road map to everywhere. This is our one map for the neighborhood, the grocery store, the United States, the whole world...thanks Mr. Pollock.

# Thank You

To my husband Rick for his love, his kindness, and his help on this book.

To my son Mike for not running away from home when he was a kid, and still loving me today.

To my friend Mary Anne Sanders for both beta reading and editing.

To my friend Mary Kalos for beta reading and editing.

To my husband Rick for editing.

To my close friends, you know who you are. Most importantly, I know who you are.

To everyone who ever followed my blog.

To everyone in every writers' group that I have ever been in and to every friend in my groups who have befriended me and are traveling this path with me.

Readers are welcome to contact me at the following email address: aspiepath@gmail.com

# Table of Contents
# Part One

# Table of Contents
# Part Two

# Preface

I started writing this book first in writers' group, then on my blog, then on my Aspie Path Facebook page.

Just like there are no books on the craft of writing that can teach you to write, there is no book about ASD or Spectrum Disorder that can teach you who and what we are. You must see us to know us. We have heightened senses and interpret the world around us differently than non-Autistic people do. That does not mean that you and I cannot communicate well: we just need to understand our differences. The only way to know us is to include us, then you will see that we are different, but not different enough to be disturbing. We are worth it just like your friendships mean so much to us.

It is far easier, and I think more accurate, for us to show you who we are than to explain it with a list of "we are," "we feel," "we are." I think to know us is to love us, but that is just me.

This book is made up of my blog posts, anecdotes from my seventy-year journey with Asperger's, and short stories from my Aspie Brain. All give you a feel of what living with Asperger's is like. Most of this journey was undertaken before there was a word for it. A strange journey it was. Most of us have additional difficulties and a life of hiding all of them the best we can from the rest of the world. Nobody but me knew that, although I have an IQ of 129, I could not learn the school bus route from school to home in twelve years. Nobody knew my anxiety every day on that bus convinced that the driver would also not know the route, and then what? I can promise you that I was not telling anyone that I did not know the route.

I was ashamed to tell anyone that I had no way of telling where my seat was in the configuration of desks, but I knew who I sat behind in every class. If the person I sat behind was absent, I stood at the back of the room until I could spot the empty seats. I am sure I always sat in the absent one's seat as even now I cannot imagine sitting behind an empty seat when I know I sit in a seat behind someone. I sit with a head in front of me.

I will share my journey with you. Some of it is sad, some of it is happy and some of it is funny.

We are an earnest and honest people, which comes through and is well done in *The Good Doctor* and *The Curious Incident of The Dog in the Nighttime.* I am also a fan of the show *Atypical*, but not all of us feel the same way about *Atypical*. I know a great many of us and respect our differences. Whatever we feel, we are always sincere. For better or worse, whatever we say is heartfelt. Now that I know that I am not the only one, which is what I thought most of my life, I would not change it. I appreciate my heightened senses and I enjoy my quirky brain.

My emotional setpoint is happy which is simply a blessing; I did nothing to deserve it, I did no work to achieve it, it is simply a gift. I am resilient like a child and in the moment like a puppy, for better or worse. We do not all share the same traits, but we share enough to strike a chord.

Frustration with not being heard, with being misunderstood is hard for us, and we do react, but so does everybody else. We just ask for the chance to be seen as people.

# Guest Blogger Rick Stein Describes Being Married to an Aspie

April 26, 2015
Being married to an Aspie
by Rick Stein

Aspie is the term some adults with Asperger's call themselves. Mari makes it sound as if it is difficult being married to an Aspie. That is far from the truth. It is the easiest and sweetest thing I have ever done. It is the most important thing I have ever done. There is a lot of information out there about Asperger's, but I only know a little. I do know a lot about Mari so that is the who I am going to write about.

Mari cannot and will never be able to drive. There is too much information flooding in all at once to be able to decode. Signs, such as ↑ mean straight ahead to most drivers: to a person who takes things literally, it means 'up'. Lanes going this way and that, people changing lanes, oncoming traffic, left turns, right turns its all too much. I would still do most of the driving even if she could drive, so she would never feel safe behind the wheel. Her driving has been a problem for her, it is not for us. Her driving would be a problem for everybody if she were on the road.

She feels uncomfortable in crowds: a lot of people do. It is not like driving, she can be in a crowd once we find a place to stay. We go to plays, movies, concerts, and fireworks displays she feels some discomfort getting there, hesitation before we go, but once we are there it is not a problem.

She will often walk behind me, she says it is because I walk too fast, but I know she is following me just as she has always done in order not to feel lost.

She is exceptionally sensitive to everything. Sensitive to touch, labels in shirts feel like thistles. She likes all her clothes to be soft. We call her the princess and the pea. Mari is sensitive to her feelings and the feelings of others. It is easy to touch a wrong nerve with her. It could only take a harsh look, a misread facial expression, ignoring her, or scaring her, to hurt her feelings or sometimes a meltdown. She will always give you a second chance, or a "do over" as she calls it. She does not stay hurt or mad for long.

There are quite a few things to learn about your partner when they are the love of your life.

We simply fit together completely and effortlessly. She laughs at my jokes, understands my unique perspective on things, loves me with all of her huge heart, takes care of me when I need it. She is smart as a whip, driven to succeed, the funniest woman I have ever met, the one woman I have ever fully trusted completely and totally with my heart. The one woman I know that has always got my back and will always looks out for me. She always has new surprises, and everything is a new surprise to her.

There is an entire book no one would read if I were to list all the reasons, I love my aspie wife.

The reasons don't really matter anyway. Love is beyond reason. It simply is that whenever I look at her, no matter what she looks like, no matter the mood she is in, no matter anything else, I see the girl I love. Before we knew anything about Asperger's Mari had the same little quirks, it is nice to have a name to call them, but it does not make any real difference to me. It's always the girl I love.

There are, to be sure, limitations that people on the Autism Spectrum have, but there are many gifts. Mari has a childlike innocence, which is a common trait of people with Asperger's. We should all wish for that same innocence. She has a sweetness about her for everyone. She talks tough when she is scared, speaks in hyperbole, can swear like a sailor, but it is just woofing to warn the danger away. Every day is fresh to her, she does not think in linear terms. Today is fresh, our trips to London and Paris are fresh, that friend from fifty years ago is fresh, A customer came into our shop one day who had been in only one time, ten years earlier and did not buy anything. She did send other people in who we did do work for in the years since. She said, "You probably don't remember me." I never would have. Mari did and told her what they had talked about, and what she was wearing.

Days do not stretch out in a long line for Mari. When she remembers something, it is like it was always just yesterday.

I am and always will be thrilled to have such a willing partner in everything. She's strong, courageous, honest, true, loving, fun, smart, sexy, interesting and interested. Who cares if she can't tell her left from her right, or that she thinks an elephant can fit in a breadbox? Who cares that she can't drive? I would drive her anywhere.

# Wedding Album

# Sensory Overload

i am growling.
they cannot hear me, but they know.
surely, they know.
they should know.
i am powerful,
they know not to approach me.
if they come too close, i will bite them.
i will bite them with my teeth.
why won't they leave me alone?
i am being still.
i will bite them if i must.
i am sad.
i am scared.
i am powerful.
i can keep them away with my growling,
my silent growling.
they know i will bite.
i hope they do not make me bite.
i hope they keep their distance.
i love them.
i hope i do not have to bite.
i am so sad.
i am so lonely.
i am so afraid.
i am so small.
all i have is the silent growl…
and the teeth.

# Other

The worst part about having Asperger's Syndrome is being "Other". I tell people that I have Asperger's Syndrome because I feel more comfortable just being myself. I would rather tell people than worry about being looked at as odd. I do not want people to regard me as peculiar. I do not know any more accurate word that explains it more clearly than "Other". We seem to be the only group where people are not embarrassed to say, "well everybody is on the Spectrum, really" or "don't we all feel that way sometimes?"

The most difficult attitude for me to deal with is that people want to re-diagnose us ."I think you have OCD." or "It's ADHD."

I think it is amazing that Psychiatrists and Psychologists spend all that time and money getting their degrees when clearly any Joe Smith on the street can diagnose OCD, ADHD, PTSD, and Autism Spectrum Disorders.

Autistic people are neurologically different. We process information differently than people who are not on the Spectrum. We refer to them as Neurotypicals because, think about it, if we refer to them as normal, where does that leave us? Nowhere good. You can be sure of that.

The simplest way to explain it is when the same information that goes into the neurotypical brain, also goes into the brain of a person on The

Autism Spectrum. The person on the Spectrum must decode it in order to understand. Sometimes this leads to sensory overload. Sensory overload is something that those of us on the Spectrum need to be prepared for, or as prepared as possible, for situations that cause a melt-down or a shut-down.

Chaos is a good word to explain what we are dealing with before a meltdown. Its synonyms: disorder, disarray, disorganization, confusion, mayhem, instability, madness, and frenzy are words that help explain how we can become overloaded by things that would not phase a Neurotypical person. I cannot read the menu at an 'order-at- the- counter' restaurant like *Panera* or *McDonald's.* It has too much information, too much space between letters, too much glaring light. Everything looks like it is in code. I really don't care that they choose not to list their sizes as small, medium and large: all I know is that within the first minute of trying to figure out how to order I am so panicked that all I want is to get the hell out of there. The overload comes at lightning speed so that I cannot read the menu board at all. It is all shine and blur and chaos. We learn very quickly not to tell the person you are with what is going on unless they know you very well because they will try to help by letting you tell them what is going on. This never ends well because what is going on is that my brain has short-circuited. All I want is to get out of there, but that is not easy either because navigating a crowded space is hard for me, when I panic it is impossible. My words are either gone, which means that I will only stare. My words are gone. I do not have them. They are gone.

When I am melting down, I conjugate the verb fuck. "Get me the fuck out of this fucking place." and it gets fancier from there. I start swearing in Spanish, which is not my native language.

I have tried so many times to explain to people what it is like, but I think it is hard to understand without experience, and if they had experience, they would be Autistic too.

People feel comfortable stereotyping us and most of them are wrong. We do not lack empathy; our social skills vary from person to person. We are not the lumbering, brooding sociopaths that many people believe us to be.

You must be on the Spectrum to hear what people say about us. Maybe your ear or sensitivities are not tuned to 'hear' when Barbara S. tells the story, on her feet with a slow staggering step, about a student she was asked to tutor. "He was so smart, but he walked like this (dimwitted slow lumber) and I was afraid of him. I couldn't have him as a student."

I really do not care about your stupidity or your insensitivity Barbara, but what other group is it acceptable to dehumanize?

I have been in several literature classes over the years and often when there is an introvert, or a character not easily understood a classmate will say "He or she is Autistic or has Asperger's. Mind you they never say that when the character is a genius, only when they are a little creepy or odd. Several times I have interrupted and said, "You don't get to do that." Clearly most people did not even hear the negative characterization. The only answer that I can think of is that it is acceptable to stereotype us, and what I say makes no impression at all. It makes me angry.

We are not broken Neurotypicals. We are Autistics, with our own strengths and weaknesses. We do not need fixing. We do not want simple awareness of us; we want awareness and acceptance.

# We're All on the Spectrum.

A nice woman named Alissa Au was a hippy-dippy kind of person, who also happened to have Asperger's Syndrome. She tired of making up reasons and excuses for her differences, so one day she jumped out of the closet and confessed. Gone were the days of saying she was tired or busy; she simply said she did not want to leave the house. She became more comfortable navigating the long way around the classroom so that she would not come upon a classmate and not know if they would step aside, run directly into her, or just stand there *forever*.

When she left the house to walk the dog, she needed to figure a way to avoid seeing anybody. The dog was a buffer, though, just in case. People could fuss over the dog; that would be okay. Certain of her well-meaning friends had remarked, "You would never know you have Asperger's Syndrome. It's hard to believe you have it."

Lissa always replied, "I hope you never see a meltdown or a shutdown. I work extremely hard to avoid it." She understood that sensory overload and the panic that ensued was hard for people to understand.

Inevitably the discussion would get around to her friends listing stereotypes, such as poor social skills and a lack of empathy.

"Well, it's a Spectrum disorder," She always said.

"When you think about it, we're really all on the Spectrum, aren't we?" Joanna begged without knowing.

"I have an idea. Would you like to see what it's like?" Alissa asked.

"You can do that?"

"Yes, Joanna, but you have to mean it."

"I mean it."

"Close your eyes, I will put my hand on your shoulder. It will take about five minutes, then I will tell you to open your eyes," Alissa said. "Open your eyes, Joanna. How do you feel? Did it take?"

"I swear," Joanna said, "there are more colors than before."

"There are, your visual senses are heightened."

"My clothes are scratchy."

"Heightened senses, but you will also feel how nicely a fine pencil glides on paper. Try it."

"That is so nice! So really, it is a gift. Damnit why did I buy scratchy clothes? What is that buzz? What is the tap tap-tap? What is the pat pat-pat?"

"Listen to the sounds around you Joanna. Those sounds are the refrigerator, the kid down the street with the basketball, the dog walking on the bed. Walk on the carpet, you will hear every step. What is happening is your brain no longer can separate out the important sounds from background noise, so you hear it all. I would strongly advise that you avoid public restrooms ... they are echo chambers with the bonus of air hand dryers. Your heart will beat so fast, and you know you cannot leave the stall until all the other people are gone. They will know you are afraid, and you will get 'that look'."

"Let's go outside, Joanna, I can give you a sense of what it's like out on the sidewalk."

"No. Is there more upside? Why are these clothes so scratchy? What was that sound?

"Yes, Joanna, there are. Your memories will be movies that you can recall virtually an eidetic memory, and you will probably be able to draw. Most of us can. Do you want to go outside?"

"No."

"No, we don't want to go outside and run into people and make small talk."

"What is small talk?"

"You used to know Joanna ... I looked it up. 'It's a polite conversation about unimportant or uncontroversial matters, especially as engaged in on social occasions."

"What? How do you do that?"

"I don't know, but it is an important social skill, and a big giveaway when we talk at the wrong time or engage earnestly, then realize that we are not having the same conversation as they are. We call them Neurotypicals, NT's for short."

"I don't know how to make small talk."

"You used to, Joanna."

"The worst part is that we need literal conversation; we misunderstand what someone is trying to tell us or asking us to do. We do what we thought they wanted, and then they get mad. They ask us to put something there. What the hell is 'something', and where is 'there'? They talk in code, then get angry when we have not pleased them. If we carry in a casserole and ask them where to put it, invariably they say 'anywhere'.

"I get it, Lissa. You make it look easy. It is exhausting, observing, and adapting second by second. All the things they do naturally, you have to work at."

"That is right." Lisa nodded, "I work at it constantly when I am in public. There is not a single moment other than when I am having a conversation with a good friend that I am not studying and working on my skills to pass for one of them."

"I'm ready for you to change me back, Lissa."

"I can't. It's okay, though, because 'we're all on the Spectrum really, remember?'"

# A Fine Eye, for Better or Worse

A memory from childhood that mystified me at the time but is kind of funny now. My family always had a nice, but small vegetable garden. One sunny weekend day Mom decided that we would each weed one row of tomatoes. One for Mom. One for Dad. One for Sis, and one for me. So, weed we did. After a while when the weeding was done.... that is, three of the rows were done, the family walked back to the start of my row and found one immaculately weeded tomato plant. There was not one single weed left around the first tomato in my row, to their eyes anyhow. I really had not finished it to perfection. Mom and Dad thought this was hilarious!!! I do not remember, but I am sure they exhorted me to speed it up. Then I looked at their rows.... rows that clearly were weeded by nearly blind people who were unable to recognize weeds.

This sad truth was driven into me throughout my childhood. The missed embroidery stitch, the crooked pictures, the mismatched silverware. My poor mother would hand me two *identical* stuffed animals, one for me and one for Sis.

"I am letting you have your choice. You always find the flaw and show me and when I cannot see it, you just stare at the flaw, then look away, then look at it again as though it will be gone. Choose carefully, and do not bring it back to me to show me," my mother would say with a scowl.

I always tried rubbing the flaw, hoping that would mitigate the horrible gaping missed stitch, discoloration, pulled thread, or whatever the flaw was. It never did. I think it is an Aspie thing. I think in pictures and cannot really understand how thinking could be otherwise.

I can spot out of square from across the room and believe I can fit anything into a drawer when I don't know where to put it. It is ridiculous, but that is how it is. Spatial anomalies are like that. I can draw upside down; all the letters work perfectly well backward for me. It is as though there is no left or right. This fine eye has served me well as an artist. Even my idiosyncrasies were well tolerated in the studio.

There is an Aspie hidden in the closet somewhere in the creation of the TV character Monk. I have never seen anybody *see* with their hands except me and Monk. Monk does the mime wall hand-walk thing, whereas I open one hand and put it by my face as though I am shielding the side of my face. What I am doing is *seeing*. I am *focusing* and *understanding*. It usually happens when I am looking at art and trying to understand someone's space in order to draw a design that will fit, or when I am on the edge of being able to visually work out a problem. This is not voluntary; I am not able to prevent it. I always apologize though because I know it is weird.

When the answer I am seeking is near, it feels the same as that moment when the magic eye picture just begins to emerge. The heart slows, there is a space, a tiny space that feels like no other. I do not know what it is, but I know that I like it every time.

# Literally

I said what I meant, and I meant what I said. An Aspie is faithful one hundred percent.

We do not lie, not about anything important. If an Aspie says, "I love you," then that is the truth. We are, for lack of a better word, guileless. I believe whatever anybody tells me, not in the carrying tales kind of way, but in the "you are my friend" kind of way. I never see personal treachery coming. *Surprise!* It is guilelessness. So, unfortunately, sometimes I get hurt and shocked on a personal level, but today the subject is about auditory incredulity.

I take things literally, and I detest the sunsa-bitchez who lie to me on the evening news, and the morning news, and on all the news. Before every commercial, there is a quiz... a quiz on the news. "Will President Obama send troops to Syria?" Well, I am sure I do not know, I kind of expected them to know, though...you know, them being in the news slot, on the news program, broadcasting the *News*. They are News*casters* no less. I find all of this extremely frustrating. I should know better by now, that this is not journalism, but it is on the news, in the news slot, so it *should* be journalism.

When I was a kid, I always asked my mom about all these *lies*. "Why did that guy on tv just say "*I wouldn't trade it for all the tea in China.*" I told her I knew he was lying, and asked: "Why did he say that?"

"Take it with a grain of salt Marianne, take it with a grain of salt."

Poor mom. That was not helpful. She always said the 'take it with a grain of salt thing' in a shrill tone that means, "I am ready to snap voice." I was a trying child, because then, pretty much like now, I want answers. Other people take these things in stride, so they must have the answers, right?

It was much easier when I was younger because the news was not quite so artful. The news was more straight forward; pretty faces reading near news and pseudo-news have replaced journalists like Walter Cronkite. We felt we could trust those journalists. We looked forward to being informed by Uncle Walter. He was family, the *smart* one in the family, and we trusted him. We loved him. The news was worth scheduling dinner around. People ate before or after the news, not during the news.

The problem is not that the newscasters cast what they cast. It is that I try to understand it every time. Then, I realize they are lying. Now I am mad, and I want *answers*! It is the same with commercials. For people who take things literally, there *are* no grains of salt.

It is not just the news. It is everywhere. Hyperbole presented as fact is pervasive. Commercials, never quite honest, now are transparent lies. What does "the best room at the best price" mean? It means nothing. The best room where? In all the world? In the slums of India? Surely not the best price in the world. Surely not the best room in all the world every-where, every day!

I do not learn, I hear it, accept it, start to move on, and then, invari-ably comes the 'what? and with that 'what?' comes frustration.

It is a big, noisy, frustrating world sometimes, and by sometimes, I mean often.

# You are Not in the Club

Sometimes I feel so childish. I was going to pose a question on Facebook (for emotional support) asking if it is ok to not include a person who is in a group with me when I do something outside the group, although many others in the group are included.

The reason I was going to pose this question is that I try to like everybody. The big downside of this is that I feel worse with every encounter with people who clearly do not like me. I have dealt with this my entire life, the glittery fixed eyes focused on me like I am something foreign that might rub off. That fake smile that makes me fear that their face will crack and fall off , don't get me wrong, after a year of trying, I don't care if her face cracks off, I just am so tired of trying to like her that I really cannot stand it anymore.

I should be immune to it by now, but it is Asperger's that she is seeing, and that obviously turns her stomach, to the point that her face freezes and her fake smile is grotesque. She must believe that I have Asperger's Syndrome *and* that I am blind. I do not know how to make that fake smile, nor do I want to know. The problem with this is that once I am done trying to be friends with someone, I am done. I don't know how to pretend, so I imagine during the next encounter, I will freeze and look like I have been hit in the back of the head with a bat, or I will drop something (which is what I did the last time).

I am seventy-three years old, and this ONE thing looks the same every time I see it. Last week I was shocked that I was over it, and it did not hurt me anymore... shocked for five minutes until that denial came and hurt more than it would have if I had admitted it to myself from the beginning. It is The Look that makes us know we are different. The look that makes us know we they see us as broken or lacking something. The look that makes us know we are unacceptable.

I do not know if this is an acceptable blog post, but I am quite sure that just like all the other feelings we have in common, I cannot be the only one who feels like this. I will feel more comfortable now not including her in 'The Club' since I have faced my sadness in this blog post.

# Bossy Miss Bossiness

# Childhood

Many adult Aspies have blogs where we write about Asperger's from our adult points of view. We write what we see and feel today. Very few of us write about what it was like to be a child without the voice to explain it through our own eyes back then. I believe that is because many of our childhood memories are colored by our misunderstanding of the people around us.

I was a young child when I first viewed my parents with distrust when they put my 15-month-old sister on the back of a horse and watched her fall off. They laughed while I melted down. At five, I realized they were irresponsible and not to be trusted. It seems my lifelong relationship with my parents was cemented in that single moment.

When I was about seven my family's Sunday visits to my dad's parents stopped. Every Sunday we would go to their house and have dinner where everybody would talk loudly. After dinner, Grandpa would sit on his chair and my dad would sit on the end of the couch adjacent to grandpa. Grandma sat in her Grandma chair, and Mom, Sis, and I sat on the couch with dad.

"No, I believe that chickens are more trouble than they're worth," my father said in a loud voice.

"That's because you are stupid," Grandpa shouted back at Dad, his only son.

"I'm not stupid, you will never get enough eggs to make them worthwhile."

"Well, you're stupid." Grandpa sang the refrain.

"If I am stupid," Dad went on, "I got it from you."

That is one of the strongest memories I have of Sundays as a child. I must have been about seven when I asked my mom why Grandpa and Dad spent every Sunday screaming at each other. She did not answer me, but Sunday dinners at Grandma's stopped.

Mom detested my grandparents, so this was a handy way to take Sundays back from my grandparents.

Dinner at home was never any better.

The family is at the table and my mother has put all the food on the table. We are sitting down and now it is time to do what they do on TV.

"How was your day?" Mom asks Dad.

Dad always has an anecdote about one of the stupid sunzabitches he works with, sometimes it is a mad anecdote, but often it is funny.

Mom asks Sis and me in turn, and we are hoping everything would be fine; that there is nothing to rock the boat. It never really mattered. It was going to be something. Maybe we were having fried potatoes and Dad would mention that nobody could fry potatoes like his Mom. This is where mom came in with her pointed but ineffective reply. Something like, "Go live at her house then."

"Well, I'm allowed to say I like my mom's potatoes," Dad said.

At this point mom was crying. She was a very emotional woman when it came to any disapproval from Dad.

I would invariably pop up with whatever positive affirmation that this situation required to avoid a fight. "You and Grandma both make good potatoes. Dad thinks you make good potatoes," or something like that. Dinner was an experience that always seemed to escalate. Frst, it would rock, and then it would shake, then it would boil, then it would churn. I could not eat much of it because I was trying to keep the peace so this would not turn into an explosion, again.

# A Nice Family Dinner

My father, Albert, sits at the head of the table. His hands are folded, eager, waiting for, in his words a "nice family dinner." His even features, light brown hair, and bright blue eyes make my father a very handsome man. He has the rough hands of a workman. It will be another 35 years before those hands grow knobby and bumpy. Filled with gout.

He is waiting for dinner, a reward for being a hard-working man. This meal is especially important because Albert's parents, my grandparents, have come for dinner.

My grandparents, Ginny, and Albert Senior are alcoholics. My mother, Dorothy-The-Protestant, makes it no secret that she considers them low-class Catholic trash. However, they are rich Catholic trash and Albert loves them both very much.

Mom is a beautiful woman. Raven haired, a little curly, and dark brown eyes that flattered her perfectly made-up face. She has grown a little rounder since she had my sister and me, but as handsome as Albert is, Dorothy still outclasses him in the looks department.

My grandparents sit side by side opposite my sister and me. My mother sits at the real head of the table because it is nearest the kitchen.

This makes it convenient for her to jump and fetch anything Albert thinks is needed to pull off the nice family dinner.

Albert watches, he's tense, waiting for something to be less than perfect. If he sees it first, he can signal mother so no one will be the wiser. He can fill in and fix any mistake that Dorothy-the-Lesser has made. He does not know that his stage whispered coaching and corrections are heard by all. Dorothy does not mind. She loves him beyond all reason. She loves him as though he is her only child and will happily spend her life making up for the shortcomings of his trashy alcoholic parents. In these situations, even more than usual, my sister and I recognize ourselves as the stage props we are.

The dinner progresses as nicely as any event can that is made up of tension held together with toothpicks and spit can be. Then, Albert notices that I am not eating. He always does. Perfect children eat their food instead of pushing it around their plates, but I cannot eat.

# Don't Look at Me

I ran away and got married at seventeen, but things went wrong long before that. An honor student rarely runs away from home, but I really did not see another way out. I had taken all the courses I needed to go to college. I had such high hopes for college.... In my plan, I would live on campus, and follow people around to get to class. To me, it seemed like a perfect environment because I love being a student and I would not have to live with my parents Al and Dorothy.

I talked to them about all my friends who were going to college, and it was virtually *all* my friends. We had been together since seventh grade when we were lucky enough to have been put into accelerated classes. We all loved learning, and it set us up with a thirst for everything that would feed our brains. We were enthusiastic and competitive in a friendly way. I had taken the languages, sciences, math as well as 4 years of English and history. The schedule was called "College Prep".

Imagine how shocked I was when my dad said, "We are not going to spend the money to send you to college. The only way would be if you were going to be a teacher or a nurse. I don't believe in sending girls to college because they wind up getting married, and it is a waste of money."

At that point not only did I realize that I was not going to college, but being unable to drive, I would be living in that house with Al and Dorothy, forever.

It was never a happy house because they liked to pretend that it was all 'Father Knows Best', but without the problems that got solved at the end of every show. They had the cosmetics down pat, a nice house, two kids and a dining room table. Right as rain and normal as can be.

I had been stewing internally since the beginning of senior year because I knew I would never be able to walk in the procession to get my diploma. I could not even return a book that I had taken from the study hall bookcase until study hall was over because I could not make myself walk in front of all the other students. Walking in front of all those people to get my diploma was never going to happen. And I could not think of a way out short of an accident or serious illness. I had no one to talk to about this, certainly not with my parents. Al and Dorothy simply wanted me to be some idealized form of a daughter. They wanted me to be normal in their eyes, and not being able to walk in the procession to get my diploma was not normal.

I decided to kill two birds with one stone and marry my boyfriend, Tom. A match made in heaven an honor student who was also a virgin, and an equally immature 19-year-old guy. What could go wrong?

After having run away together and a few days in jail in Atlanta, Georgia, waiting for Tom's dad to pick us up and drag us home, we started our married life.

Mom was furious. She said, "Not only did you deprive us of seeing you walk down the aisle to get married, you have deprived us of seeing you get your diploma."

That walking down the aisle terrified me, that was never going to happen.

I only had to not go to college and marry the wrong guy to achieve my goal.

# Suicide is Not About a
# Temporary Problem

Suicide, by its very nature, is a lonely, solitary business. It seems Robin Williams' suicide struck a sharper chord in me than any of the accidental overdoses of other celebrities.

"Suicide is a permanent solution to a temporary problem." Celebrity doctors like Drew Pinsky are all over the airways making an effort to send the message that the depression is temporary, that there are better days ahead, but when you're *there*, and I have *been there,* you know that those who counsel patience have not been in that black, bleak spiral of hopelessness. The popular statement, his message, however, is of value to people who are sad, who *will* have brighter days ahead.

Teens, with their rampant hormones and emotions, sometimes try on Emo and Goth personas. Those who have not really *seen* it, think it is deep, romantic, and glamorously tragic. It is none of those and it is not a good suit to try on.

Pema Chodron, America's first and most respected Buddhist nun, teaches us not to "bite the hook", to not to engage with and be ruled and hurt by our triggers. I understand it and I get it. I am pretty good at it, but she also teaches us to "sit with the pain". I understand that. The lesson is, when you sit with the pain, and you sit it out all the way through, you will come out the other side knowing that neither grief, nor pain, nor sadness will kill you.

I have never been able to do that. I mentioned it to my sister, and she said she has never been able to do that either. Those of us who are still alive and cannot "sit with the pain," drink or reach for the helpful tranquilizer to keep us from running into a wall.

I wonder, because Robin had been treated for addiction so many times, if he too was unable to "sit with the pain".

The point of this essay is my belief that depression is more organic than emotional, and because of this, it cannot be treated only with logic or words.

My suicide risk is low because I do not engage much with pain. I cannot afford to, but those with both a biological predisposition and an inability to head the dark thoughts off at the pass and have realized the excess of drink and drugs will kill them anyway, are at a monumental risk.

# A Day at the Park

It was a warm, breezy day. The trees were impossibly tall and swaying in the forest. Not a scary kind of swaying, but the gentle movement of nature that signified a perfect day, well not a perfect day because extra people had come along to this picnic in Cook Forest.

Jill and her mom were there. I did not know why. Jill was a some-times friend, depending on what her mysterious, beautiful mom was doing. This day they were doing a picnic with us. Jill was a grade younger than my little sister Rosy. She was seven, Jill was six and I was ten.

I am Dory. I had a secret. Nobody knew that there were a lot of things that I could not do. Some of those things even the little kids could do better, but nobody seemed to notice. I was afraid that I would get found out, and that there would be trouble, or that people would laugh at me, which was a different kind of trouble.

One of the things I could not do was find my way, anywhere. I was always lost, and I tried not to go anywhere by myself. That was a secret. I was ashamed.

The day at the picnic started out ok. We were going to have ham-burgers and baked potatoes like we always had. I loved how we set out the onions, the relish, the ketchup, and the buns. Only my mom knew how to make the onions right. Everybody else made the pieces too big. The hamburgers, which always seemed to take forever would be piled on a big plate. They would be big and fat with uneven edges, grey, drippy, and delicious.

Then it happened, I was always on the watch for this type of thing. Mom asked if I would take the little kids down to the lake. "What lake?" I thought. "Where would t a lake be in the forest? Oh, she must have said *water.*"

"Will you take the little kids down to the water?" my mother repeated.

Rosy and Jill were both excited and wanted to go, so I whispered to her, "Do you know the way?" She nodded. She and Jill darted down to the water. I followed in hot pursuit. I was happy seeing them have a good time, but I was lost and would not feel easy until we were all back at the picnic. Until we made it back, from my point of view, we were all lost. I did a really good job of watching them and making sure that they did not get hurt. I was good at that. I always looked out for my little sister. I was protective of her because I felt my parents were unfit to raise children. They were careless. This was another thing I kept secret.

The kids played for a while until it was time to go back to the picnic. Mom had said, "Don't be too long." I knew that meant we should be there when the food was ready. We started back, and all was looking good. And then... "I forgot my barrette." Jill wailed. She insisted that it had to be found, so they wanted to go back. I just neeed the little kids to lead us back to the picnic. I asked Rosy if she knew the way back to the water and back to where I was waiting. She said she did.

I see that I should not have let them go alone. I was ashamed that I did not know the way. I waited and waited for them to come back. I waited so long that I thought the little kids were already back at the picnic. I walked and walked and there they were.... Mom and Jill's mom. I had found my way back to the picnic! I expected to see the little kids too.

"Where is Jill, where is Jill?" her mom screeched. "You lost my daughter," she hissed "This is all your fault."

"How could you lose the little kids? Oh God, where are the little kids, Dory?" Mom screamed.

The screaming seemed to go on forever. I had no words; I was not really there. My head was swimming and my eyes were unfocused. My heart pounded in my ears. Shortly, Rosy and Jill came back, but I do not remember anything about the rest of the day.

# Sensitive Hearing, it's Not Just for Vampires Anymore

I have heard remarks about my sensitive hearing my whole life. "Oh, yes, Marianne hears everything." That was my mother's lament. Most of my unusual traits set her teeth on edge. I guess life with me must have been like living with an odd little ghost for her. My niece dubbed it 'Vampire Hearing' but, unlike my mother, she finds it fascinating. She finds *me* fascinating.

The worst thing about hypersensitive hearing is that sounds are scary. When someone is walking behind me on the sidewalk, I get scared. Scared enough that I move to the side so they will pass me, and they WILL pass me because I will not move again until they are well ahead. That does not quite describe it, though. When someone is approaching me from the side, usually in a big store, I can hear them, and I turn my head away from them in order not to see them because I am already scared. Then the suspense of when or whether they will pass me heightens my stress. If I cannot stand the stress anymore, I turn my head just enough to get an idea of who is there. Sometimes it makes it better, and sometimes it makes it worse. If it is a tall and hefty being, it makes it considerably worse, because I will not lift my eyes to see the face. The face might be nice, but I am not taking that chance. I will react badly if I lift my eyes and see 'resting bitch face'. I am already scared and ready to escape. I want to go home.

Today I bought some Bluetooth noise-canceling earbuds. Because they are Bluetooth, nobody will know that there is likely no audio, just less noise. I have a fear of being regarded as crazy. It is unwise to be different from the tribe. Getting people to stop walking behind me would be a big step in the right direction.

Crowds and chaos and noise, oh my. Where I live there seems to be no such thing as an inside voice or even a taboo against urinating on a toilet seat. These two things may seem unrelated, but they are not. They show a lack of civility, moreover, they show a complete lack of concern or awareness for others. I grant that my Asperger's Syndrome causes me to hear sounds more acutely than most other people, but I do not understand why people who are out in public choose to speak in the same volume that they use in their own living rooms. Maybe I do know, maybe it is because they feel the need to talk over the rest of the people in the restaurant who are speaking voce forte least one word of their impressive conversation be lost. We might never know how important they are. They might become invisible in the din.

The lack of civility, the lack of awareness, of a standard of consideration necessary to society convinces me that if I do not leave, my head will fall off. Call it sensory overload if you must, it is not all the Aspie's doing. It is not always the Aspie's fault for not tolerating the intolerable.

# Why I Don't Bake Cookies

I don't often bake cookies; I never did. They take forever, and the dirty bowls, measuring cups and spoons are just not worth seeing the pleasure on my family's faces for the 20 minutes it takes to devour forty-eight cookies.

As always, I am in the lead. Only I know that I have already eaten so many cookies, because I ate all the imperfect ones. That's why I have to make sixty cookies, it's just not acceptable to offer imperfect cookies. It is not acceptable to bake imperfect cookies. People will hold me in a lower regard if they ever find out the secret to making perfect cookies is eating the bad ones. Nobody will like me. Ever.

I make every cookie perfectly, no rough edges as I use the 2-tea-spoon method, scoop, scrape, smooth the top peak nicely with the back of the spoon. Twelve cookies perfectly spaced on the cookie sheet.

Ten minutes later I take the misshapen mess out of the oven. How, HOW I ask you, can the perfectly shaped cookies have crawled into the edges of the baking sheet? As I look at the 8 good cookies and the 4 cook-ies with delicate square edges that will crumble raggedly as I remove them from the baking sheet, I resolve to proceed with the rolled round ball method. I roll each piece of cookie dough into a perfectly round ball, 1 inch in diameter. As I place 12 perfectly spaced cookies on the baking sheet, I am hopeful. I truly believe that there will be 12 perfect cookies in 10 minutes.

As I remove the cookies from the oven, I notice that, while none of them are terrible, none of them are very good, either...a little over-baked with really burnt spots on the bottom of the edge ones...I hate having to eat burnt cookies!

I would love to bake 9 cookies on a sheet, but they don't make square baking sheets, so there you go....

At this point I have 8 good cookies and 4 passable cookies, an even dozen so far.

I will use 2 baking sheets and put 6 cookies on each sheet now that I have rerolled all the cookie dough into 1 ½" balls. Keeping them away from the edges is the key. I will have a dozen perfect cookies in 10 minutes.

Ten minutes later I find that the larger cookies, kept well away from the edges have contentedly spread into each other. Of course, the edges where they are stuck together have broken as I removed them from the baking sheets. Ten reasonably good cookies from this batch, only 2 to eat, but they are big ones.

Twenty-two decent cookies. If I proceed with the big cookie plan I will eventually have 48 decent cookies, I just know it!

Two pans of 6 cookie yield another 10 passable cookies. Two big cookies to eat, and I have 32 cookies, this crap is getting old. I am going to make 16 more cookies by re-rolling the balls to make 16 cookies, I may have to roll them more than once to get them all the same size, but I will prevail.

Cookies rolled, placed on pans, 2 pans of 8 cookies each, bake for 10 minutes. I will clean all the mess from cookie baking and make sure that all the bad cookies have been eaten so there will be NO evidence of my imperfect cookies, so no signs will remain of my failure as a cookie baker.

I hear the timer and hopefully open the oven door. So far so good. They look like cookies. There will be 48 passable cookies for dessert, nobody will be the wiser.

I hadn't baked cookies in almost 20 years, but it all came back to me when my niece asked me to bake cookies for her High School's annual bake sale.

I fretted a bit and found myself mortified at the possibility of failure. I have an exaggerated fear of failure. Whenever someone complimented me and used the word perfect, I would invariably reply "Well, my motto is *Perfect or Dead.*" I seemed to be kidding but in reality, no. I am not kidding.

That evening, almost 20 years after my final cookie baking attempt, I resolved to not disappoint my niece, so after a trip to Costco we are 48 cookies to the good. As I remove them from their noisy cheap plastic packaging, I smile and carefully arrange them in the absolutely perfect size Tupperware container. I line them up straight and true and ding them up some so they will look homemade.

# Recovering My Voice

I have not written anything worthwhile for a long time. This morning I understood why. I lost my voice, not my physical voice, but I lost that too. The vocal cord is going to be "pumped up" by a fifteen-minute surgery one week from today, but that is not the voice that matters. I lost my voice; I lost me. What replaced me was cancer. I have been genuinely bewildered by what has happened to my body. Chemotherapy knocked back the cancer, but it also took three months of my life to recover from the side effects. It even took my near vision, which was a big deal to me. I was heartsick enough to give away my books. I moderate drawing classes at our local Lifelong Learning Institute. How was I to do that when I could not see to draw or critique? I was advised to get magnifying glasses. It just does not work that way. It simply does not. After all these months my near vision finally came back. I was jubilant.

About a week later I got what I thought was laryngitis, but it was not laryngitis. I could drink several sips of water (Gatorade) but then inevitably my throat would close and force me to spit it out. This was followed directly by a coughing fit. I waited three weeks, thinking I could ride out this laryngitis.

Just by luck, my oncologist called to set up an appointment to discuss immunotherapy options for me if this cancer started to grow. I was self-conscious about my squeaky fading voice, so I said "laryngitis". He set me up with the ENT so here we are. This is where we are today. Today.

I have always had a "gift" for living in the moment. I lost that. I lost myself.

Cancer, the fear of making the cancer "angry" has been running my life. I feel like it is a sleeping egg. "Don't wake it. Do not fall and jar it, do not wake it. Don't make it mad."

This Stops Today! Today and tomorrow and every tomorrow after that. I will live my life.

Being ashamed of how I look and staying in the house is an impractical and unhappy solution. I accept that it will take a while to accept my chemo-ugly hair and my too-pale skin, at the least I will stop posting selfies looking for affirmation.

Today I lost my friend, Shawnee Lewis, to cancer. Her struggle was long and hard, but she was always whole. She was always Shawnee. I intend to be me from now on. I am going to do what I want. I think we need a trip to NYC to get some of Ray's Pizza. I grew up in an Italian town, and I need pizza, Real pizza.

When the time comes, my husband Rick has promised to spread my ashes on the grounds of every pizza parlor in Youngstown, Ohio. So back to today and every today after this. I hope to be and will be more entertaining in my next post.

Love you guys,

Aspie Path

# Social and Logistics

Seventh-grade year was when my school decided to group the brightest students together to offer a more challenging curriculum. We loved it! Back then there was no such thing as a "gifted child". We were just "The Brains" from seventh grade through high school. We had a ready-made clique that suited us.

I especially loved junior high. At last, I was not the only one with boobs as I had been since the 5th grade. We had our own little separate space, and the same kids were in every class.

The junior high was only separated from the senior high by a long ramp. Both that long ramp and the high school kids were Off Limits. The high school kids were also warned not to even step on that ramp. I loved it!

High School was much more difficult for me logistically. All the cracks in my coping skills could get wider and show more. It was nerve wracking trying to find my classes. The building itself was huge to me at the time. Every door in every hallway looked the same. I would never ask for help because I would have died from embarrassment to be found out. Luckily, my friends in the advanced classes knew where they were going, and I always followed them.

It was the same problem with the school bus. I had to find someone who rode my bus so I could get on the right one. I would be lost forever if that happened and there was no scenario in which I would confess that I was indeed lost. I could not learn the bus route home in twelve years, nor could I spot my house when the bus driver ran the route backward. From the moment he announced the 'backward route' my stomach was in knots as I thought "maybe this time I will be able to see the house" so I will know where my stop is. But that never happened.

It is still the same today. I can walk the 3 blocks to our neighborhood plaza, but it is a straight path. I know a few of the neighbors, but I can only recognize their houses if they are standing in the yard, otherwise, all the houses look the same to me.

Nothing about this is has ever been easy.

# Autism Journal page 6, 7, 6A, or the other 6... depending on whether I am numbering pages consecutively or repetitively

People with Autism Spectrum Disorder see and understand the world differently. The truth is that we run on a different operating system. Our system can work well enough with most of the OS out there, and integrate pretty well with the world, but like Linux, Mac, and Windows, the integration is far from seamless.

It is time that I stop referring to these differences as problems, implying that all can be solved and resolved. It will have to be OK as it is.

The puzzle piece, as the symbol for autism awareness, is neither good nor bad. It is, however, not accurate. It seems so much is in code, a code that I do not have the key to. Every day, people with ASD run into situations that are hard for us to understand. It is often extremely hard to comprehend and interpret what we see and hear. Most of us are very fearful of making other people mad with our responses or, more accurately, our lack of compliance. It is the "different operating system" thing. We often have a hard time understanding what is expected of us. Communication problems are common enough to be daunting.

For example, I used to think that everything regarding the "sketch artist" whether on TV or reported on the news was an elaborate lie, because I knew full well that without many encounters, context of those encounters, voice familiarity and a whole string of necessary repetitions it would be impossible to recognize people , having only seen them once, let alone describe them for the sketch artist. It was only after I understood that Aspies are different that I could sort of accept that other people can do these things, like recognize people they have only met once.

I am so lucky that I can embrace interpersonal relationships, make friends and be empathetic. This is somewhat more common in women on the Autism Spectrum than in men, however Dan Aykroyd, one of our better-known men on the Spectrum, seems to do well. BBC's Sherlock has Asperger's syndrome. Monk as played by Tony Shalhoob is obviously on the Spectrum, as is the annoying Sheldon Cooper on Big Bang Theory. It is no longer the mysterious/closet disorder that it once was.

Women sometimes fare better socially than men with ASD. That is most likely because we are better mimics. Women have a better ability to watch and learn how to be. I especially value this ability, because I sincerely believe that The TRIBE will gleefully kill and eat the ones who are different. I do not know if this belief is from 'the collective unconscious' or just a belief deeply rooted in my own soul, but to me it is a truth.

Modern medicine is a godsend. The anti-anxiety medications make it much easier for me to function in this bright, loud world where it seems to me that the stranger coming at me with the shopping cart in the Kroger, will at a minimum, maim me. It takes about 15 minutes until I hate all these loud strangers with their noisy kids and murderous shopping carts. Again, this results in me cursing in Spanish.

The bright lights, the CH-CH-CH-AHHH from the air compressors, the buzzing fluorescent lights, the tick-tick- buzz-ding of the cash register and the whoosh of the entry doors accompanying the squeaky-metallic sounds of the shopping cartwheels remind me that normal is not coming anytime soon.

# No, I Don't Drive

The way that Asperger's Syndrome has affected my life the most is not being able to drive. This is a hard concept for people to understand. Everybody can drive.

"Oh, of course, you can drive, everybody can drive."

"You just lack confidence, once you get out there, you will see how easy it is. You are so smart, of course, you can drive, idiots can drive."

Recently, I had a conversation with a health worker when my husband Rick was in the hospital five days after heart surgery. I explained that we would be waiting for our ride to take him home. "Well you're driving him home, right?"

"No, I don't drive."

"Well, how did you get here?"

"A friend brought me."

"But you used to drive, didn't you? You just don't drive anymore, right?"

"No, I never drove, I have Asperger's Syndrome. I think every sign in sight is an instruction for me. Sensory overload."

"But you used to drive, right?" This time with a teasing smile.

"No, I did *not* 'used to drive'. What part of this do you think is funny?"

"I don't think it's funny."

"No, but you think I *used to drive,* and you think I don't drive now because I am afraid. Do I seem like a sissy to you?"

"No."

"That's right, NO!"

I 've had many too many variations of that conversation in my life and I am tired of it.

I do not understand how anybody *can* decipher the traffic sign code. Stop. No Right Turn on Red. Wrong-Way. Do not enter. Left Turn Signal. Yield. Wrong way. Wrong way. Wrong way.

It looks like this to me every day. Every single day. A lot of spaces look like this to me.

Driving a 3000-pound vehicle powered by gasoline, on the road, in traffic does not seem like the smart move to me.

Not being able to drive has affected my life profoundly. There is no doubt that I would not have run away from home at 17 if I could drive. I had graduated from high school at the top of my class. I had taken all the college prep classes because I thought I was going to college, like all my friends. I could not see any way to fulfill my dreams without going to college. I had no intention of growing old with my parents. I did not want to be the family spinster. My nineteen-year-old boyfriend proposed to seventeen-year-old-me. I married him. In 1965, there were no other options that I could see.

# We are Brave

People on the Autism Spectrum have both gifts and challenges, but bravery is our superpower. Getting up every day to participate in a world that does not understand us, and that we do not understand is hard. We are brave.

It is hard when we say "thank you" to a remark that was sarcasm, then get laughed at. It is hard when it happens again and again because we never see it coming no matter how many times it happens. We are brave.

We each have the right to avoid those situations. We keep trying, though. That is bravery. Believing that we are somehow deficient and thinking that it is our fault that we receive that treatment because we 'should have learned by now' makes that uphill battle even harder. We are brave.

Each of us has to decide for themselves how to handle our challenges. The world is not going to change for us. We are not able to, and would not want to, give up our place on the spectrum. Think about it, we did not get Autism. We were born this way. Each of us gets up every day and engages with the world in some way, while we know full-well that trying to fool the dominant tribe of Neurotypicals isn't going to work because humans are tribal, and we don't fool ourselves. We know they can spot us, and day after day we engage with a world that does not understand us. We are brave.

Every one of us knows that it is not safe to be different. We are different, though, and navigating this world is necessary. It is not about fitting in, it is about living in the world as ourselves and making the best of our strengths and skills. We have value. It is about recognizing we give value to our friends and family, to our work and to our communities.

We are brave. Bravery is our superpower.

# Nothing About This Is Easy
# Part Two

STORIES
Mostly True

JoDean doing her best, like we do,
all day every day.

# JoDean

# Sadly She's Gone

Mari Stein is gone. She would have written her own eulogy had she known that we needed it well before 12:16 PM February 15, 2023. She could always meet a deadline, but only when her back was against the wall, and she didn't know she was going.

Mari always said she wanted to leave nothing undone when she died. When I told her I felt that was impossible, she said, "No, every day I want my husband Rick to know how much he is loved, admired and appreciated. I want him to know that I *know* he is my rock, my biggest fan, my best cheerleader. I want my son Michael to know that he has been a joy every day from the day I first met him, my little olive skinned, blue eyed baby with 2 inches of black hair carefully coaxed into a rooster's comb. Michael looking both innocent and serious from his first day on this earth. I want him to know every day how very proud I am of him. And my closest friends, I want them to know that I cherish their friendship, kindness, and support.

A friendship not nurtured, a kindness not acknowledged, an admiration not expressed, Mari felt would lead to an unfinished life.

Every day was a new day for her. She never became inured to anything, for better or for worse. The silver-grey green color of kale was incredibly beautiful every time she saw it. The river "sparkled like diamonds" every time. Every time was the first time in the sense that it was viewed with the same vast appreciation....or abhorrence. There was no middle ground. She was happy like a child, and hurt like a child. She never saw it coming... the anger, the disdain... and she took it right to heart. This led to anger (mainly at herself ) for her lack of emotional maturity. With that anger came the outrage of a six year old, the deep hurt that is only possible for someone who lacked the ability to be as inured to pain as she was to pleasure.

So she's gone for now.

I know she expects to be back soon. She often raised her eyebrows and said," I will return as a dung beetle in my next life." Whether as Bodhisattva, "to dispel the miseries of the world", or as a new person with another journey on this earth, she knows she will be back, whether her mission is to learn or to help. She will be back.

# Perception

The Art Glass Trade Show of 1990 was held in Cincinnati. Six other stained-glass pattern book artists and I had agreed to share a booth. It was a good space where we all could sell and autograph our pattern books. It was convenient for the convention visitors to be able to meet all the artists and buy books in one location.

I had made it clear, back in 1985 when all of the designers were kicking around the idea of having booths for the next Trade Show, that I would not participate if we each had to have our own booth. The center of attention is a place that terrifies me. At that time, I was extremely well known in my little pond, but I got to stay in my own space and work designing patterns in my own studio. At home.

An especially good thing was that we could break for lunch whenever we wanted, because another artist would cover our book sales. I had just left the booth when the actress who played "Mama" in the movie *Throw Mama From the Train,* was clearly heading right for me. Wait... does she wear an eye patch? I think she was in *Goonies* too, and there were pirates in *Goonies.* so I was convinced that yes, it was that actress. Within seconds she took my hand in both of hers and said, "I really admire your work." She was standing *way* too close, holding my hand and it was not that actress.

It was a man, a man with an eyepatch who looked exactly like her. I was not used to and didn't *like* to have strangers stand so close to me, and I did not like having my hand captured by the two hands of this stranger. I removed my hand and said, "Thank you very much, but I have to get back to work." I went directly back to the Designers' booth.

Two years later one of my favorite customers came into our stained-glass studio carrying a copy of Smithsonian Magazine.

"I  brought this for you." he said. "This month's issue has an article about your idol, Dale Chihuly. There are lots of pictures too."

"Thanks a lot ! I am really excited to see it." I waited until after he left to open the magazine.

"Oh my god! What have I done? It's the lady from *Throw Mama From the Train.*"

I called my favorite stained-glass distributor and confessed. I told her I felt like an awful person.

She said, "Good for him, he thinks he's too good to talk to anyone."

I still felt awful and called my son and told him what I had done.

He said, "You know, he went back to his friends and said, *"and you said she was so nice!"*

He laughed until I laughed too.

# One Angry Redhead

After a perfect anniversary dinner at Carrabba's where we dined on spaghetti and margherita pizza, Rick and I headed home. It was Halloween. Trick or Treaters would likely be coming to our door, so we stopped and bought candy for the little goblins and witches. We were almost home. Three houses from our driveway, a truck was sitting in the middle of the road. Initially, we thought the people, badly parked, were waiting for their own little masqueraders to come back and get in the truck. They were there much too long, though for that to be the case; they kept sitting there instead of backing up and parking against the curb so that other cars could pass.

"What are they doing?" I asked.

"Just sitting there," said Rick.

I noticed that the person in the passenger seat was casually sipping a beverage from a can.

"This is not working for me, I'm jumping out." At this point my door was already halfway open.

I walked up to the truck and said, fairly patiently, "Back up so we can pass."

He said, "No you back up."

In a calm voice, I said, "Get out of your truck and look. You will see that you are in the middle of the road."

The driver sneered at me and said, "I know. I know where I am."

I said, "Back the fuck up."

The driver said, "No you back up, you guys came running up on me all aggressive."

I said, "Back the fuck up."

The driver said, "No."

At this point, I added both Italian hand signals and traffic cop hand gestures to my profane 'back up' refrain. Such a sight it must have been, a feisty 5' tall redhead mad as a wet hen. Furious. Steely-eyed and serious as a heart attack.

Alarmed by the ruckus, our curious neighbor, Shirley, came out on her porch.

"Oh, for God's sake! Back up, Danny. This is my neighbor, Mari."

Danny said. "NO."

"This is my son," Shirley said, "I'm sorry."

"Danny, pull in here," she said.

Danny pulled into her driveway.

"Shirley said, I am so sorry. He's my son."

I said, "It's ok."

I got back in the truck and turned to Rick. "We know him, don't we?"

Rick said, "Yeah, he's always an ass."

"I remember now," I said.

# Miss McKendry's No Science
# 7th Grade Science Class

The worst teacher I ever had, indeed the worst teacher I ever saw, was Miss McKendry. She was 4 feet 9 inches of pure crazy. We knew this not only from her reputation of jumping off her desk, but I knew it from those eyes. Her eyes glittered with unfounded excitement. The first day of class we wondered how long it would be until she jumped. I, for one, wanted that to be a myth. I hoped it was an untruth enjoyed and perpetuated by each classes to titillate the next class. Everybody loves an "in" joke; Miss McKendry was the perfect foil, but she proved the myth to be true.

The first week of class she climbed on the chair and up onto the desk. There she made some noise asserting that humans cannot fly, even if they flap their arms. So, there she is, tight grey curls badly contained on her elderly head, crazy eyes looking directly at her captive audience, while trying to raise onto her toes. The thick heels of her heavy black oxfords made quite a task of it, but she didn't let that stop her. She had been doing this bimonthly for more years than anyone could count. She mustered enough lift to carry her off the desk and as she landed on the floor she said, "Humans can't fly."

The other thing she did that first week was give us our ONE and only assignment for the year. We were to collect fall leaves for class. They had to be "perfect" leaves, not small, not large, not spotted, not curled." Only perfect leaves would qualify. I drove my mother crazy obsessing about my leaves not being perfect enough. This was for a GRADE.

Miss McKendry loved to teach standing on her desk. She was my homeroom teacher and one of two science teachers for the 7th grade. It was my misfortune to have her as a teacher instead of the real science teacher. I absolutely detest crazy for the sake of crazy, and that is exactly what we were dealing with. We had science books; we could have spent that 50 minutes each day studying science. Studying directly from the books. It would have required no effort on her part. She could have made up test questions directly from the review in each section. We could have had Science Class. Instead we had a woman instructing us on "men with value vs. men without value."

"My father was a wonderful man," she raised her eyes, her face glowed with a beatific smile. Then she launched into a tribute about her father's military heroism. She was too old to be teaching, so I could never really understand when his military career took place, but it didn't matter because from there she launched into a diatribe about men who did not serve in the military. I think this diatribe covered any and all wars. "Namby Pambies" they are. Panty Waists, I say. They are not worth my father's pinkie finger!" As she said this she had her hands on her hips and minced around, back, and forth on the desk.

As she got angrier over these 'Nambie Pambies', she adopted her Shirley Temple voice and a five-year-old child's earnestness. She drew her elbow back then thrust her fist forward and upward in an awkward hooray kind of motion. It was as confusing as it was disturbing.

I for one hated it. I hated it every day. It is not like we ever went to class and had a science lesson. We no longer had those expectations, but as a person who values order and routine, I detested never knowing what each day's crazy was going to be.

Of course, we all got B's on our report cards. The class kept asking when we should turn in our leaves. "Not yet," she would say, She never wanted them. She changed her mind.

# Me Llamo Manuel

"Welcome to the Caño Negro river tour. Me llamo Manuel. I am the leader of this albino monkey troupe. My troupe and I, in my humble opinion are the stars of this tour. Ah, here comes our friend Jorje, he is the human guide on the tour. We see him every day. I speak 2 languages, Monkey and Eengleesh. I learned all my human language by listening to Jorje, my tour guide partner."

"Manuel, it's the pirates! why do the pirates come every day?"

"I told you, Camila, these are not pirates these are tourists. We have no pirates on this river."

"The parrots told me they are pirates, and that the parrots ride around on the pirates' shoulders, and the pirates said they are going to take us across the river to Nicaragua. To Nicaragua where they eat monkeys!"

"Camila, I think you don't speak such good Parrot, and in any case, I have heard that they have wild imaginations and enjoy making up stories. The parrots are very jealous because they are a minor part of the tour. Go hide if it makes you happy, just remember that nobody will take your picture then. We are a small troupe. It is nice to have all of us in the photo."

"Hi Jorje, I am ready," said Manuel.

"This small troupe of albino or blonde monkeys are a rare muta-
tion," Jorje began as did on every tour as they approached. "Like all howler
monkeys, they eat mostly leaves, then rest to digest them. Their best diet is
the new young leaves at the tips of the branches that they can reach when
they hang by their prehensile tails."

"Here I go, Jorje."

"Oh look," one of the tourists says, "that one is stretched out and
hanging by its tail! It's eating the tiny new leaves."

"Got your back Jorje."

"That monkey, I call him Manuel. He is the leader of this troupe
of rare monkeys. He is very smart and handsome, no? Due to inbreeding,
though, they are all sterile."

"What does sterile mean Manuel?" said Camila.

"I don't know *all* the Eengleesh words, but I think it has to do with
the nighttime stars, Camila. I think it is another way of saying how special
we are. Move about and do monkey stuff but stay close to the river so the
tourists can see us. We are. after all the stars of the whole tour."

"Jorje is ready to ride further down the river to show them the sloths
way up in the trees, although, in my opinion, they are completely indistin-
guishable from clumps of leaves. Good tour, Jorje. See you tomorrow,"
said Manuel.

# Pura Vida

What nobody told me when Rick and I planned a trip to Costa Rica, is that Costa Rica, instead of being about sloths, monkeys, and iguanas, is about Pura Vida. Pura Vida… damned right, exactly...all positive, all the time. Life is good, the people are good, the food is good. It is a place apart. "Pura Vida", is like the 'hippie handshake'. It never fails to elicit an enthusiastic "Pura Vida" right back. "Con mucho gusto", (with much pleasure) is the consistent response to "gracias". See the difference? In high school Spanish, we were taught "de nada", (it's nothing) was a proper response to gracias, but how much more gracious, how telling the attitude of the Ticos, "with much pleasure".

After a few hours, the rhythm of the country is contagious. Costa Rica really is about the people, the Ticos. The Cano Negro Tour where we saw enormous orange iguanas and small orange monkeys who are called blonde or albino, as well as swifts who followed the boat and ate mosquitos would not have been as impressive without our local guide, Gorge, who told us those birds have glands that attract the mosquitoes, or of the impending extinction of the troupe of albino monkeys who are now sterile due to inbreeding.

Gorge gave us a brief history of Costa Rica including that 25% of the national economy is derived from tourism and that the country gave up their standing army in 1949 and have chosen instead to fund free primary and secondary education for all the children. Costa Rica boasts a literacy rate of 96%. It is an eco-friendly country named the greenest country in the world in 2009, and in 2012, they banned recreational hunting. The U.N settled a dispute in favor of Costa Rica regarding the river that runs between Costa Rica and Nicaragua. Nicaragua wants to dig a canal that will cause irreparable damage to Costa Rica's ecosystem. Gorge feels that, sadly, Nicaragua will not give up their push for a canal. On this river tour we saw many birds and we were lucky enough to see a green heron. The hoped-for views of sloths would have to wait for another day as they were so high in the trees that they appeared to be clumps of leaves.

Our kinkajou night walk was also a guided tour. Our guide Alex was an enthusiastic and capable guide. He led us to areas of the forest in Monte Verde to where we were able to see two types of pit vipers, many sleeping birds, nocturnal mammals, and a 2-toed sloth carrying her brown baby on her stomach. We watched the sloth for quite a while, as she moved through the branches and even went from tree to tree. We did a lot of hiking to see all the wildlife and Alex was good at noticing that Marianna needed some help scaling the steeper hills.

He would occasionally ask "where is Marianna?"

I would say "here". Again, the guide added to the experience.

In Manuel Antonio, it was much hotter than in Monte Verde, and the Manuel Antonio Park was full of monkeys, small iguanas, and apparently crocodiles. "No Alimentes Los Cocodrilos" signs were present, and the part of the trail that connected the loop was closed due to El Corcodilos. The new route stopped at the beach and backtracked, which meant more wonderful and curious monkeys. Every creature in Costa Rica is appreciated and respected for its importance to the ecosystem.

Pura Vida! I felt better those eight days in Costa Rica than I have ever felt in my life. A diet of gallo pinto, eggs, fruit, seafood, and Imperial (Costa Rica's popular beer) just works. A clean environment filled with wonderful people and beautiful nature made me realize how important genuine environmentalism is. It made me realize the importance of clean eating as well. I didn't know that fried food is the devil until I found out how good I felt when I didn't eat it.

Before we visited, I heard that all they eat is rice and beans for every meal. Gallo Pinto is *not* rice and beans, well technically it is, but really, it isn't. It is *Costa Rican* rice and beans. They are significantly different from Mexican rice and beans or Cuban rice and beans, or New Orleans red beans and rice. Gallo Pinto is drier and plausible as an all-purpose side dish. My favorite breakfast is gallo pinto, scrambled egg, and fruit. Lizano sauce is Costa Rica's brown sauce that some people like to add at the table, sort of like putting ketchup on potatoes.Rick and I carried the clean eating home, for a while anyway. It's probably time to go on another Costa Rican vacation again.

# Present-day Snow and a Memory
# of Christmas Past

Mari Stein 2019

Today is a perfect day. A richly saturated light blue sky holds its own above fluffy white clouds that mimic the untouched snow below. The trees, supporting heavily scattered clumps of wet snow, easily support the burden. Everything is clean and new on this first snow day. New snow, reflecting the sun, sparkles like diamonds and makes everything brighter. Snow reflects the sun in the winter eliciting feelings of well-being in much the same way as sand's brightness at the ocean. It's cheerful.

At Hilton Head, or anywhere that there is white sand, beach photos often look like snowscapes, and unlike snow, it stays white year-round. Neither is a good choice for me year-round, but I would rather deal with the cold than live year-round in sun so bright that it burns your eyes and blisters your feet. So, as anybody can see, Hilton Head is the perfect place in the winter. It has great beeches, the ocean, it is a perfect temperature for me, and it is NOT crowded.

It was a culture shock the first year we went to Florida during the Christmas holiday. I thought and sort of still do that Christmas lights are unnecessary where it's sunny year-round.

It is a good thought though, to keep the tree up year-round for cold grey days and rainy days during the winters up north.

As soon as I see snow on the trees I am eager to put up our own decorated and lighted tree. I never considered a decorated tree to be any kind of symbol of Christianity because Santa is the symbol of the season. When I was a child, he brought the tree the night before Christmas and decorated it. As I understand it, Santa is an independent contractor who works for milk and cookies, so the tree is a sweet deal! As I learned it, he also brought some kind of gift, maybe based on whether you have been good or bad, but most likely depending on what type of parents you have. Even Santa has a limit. If your family leaves a note suggesting a not-a-Barbie-doll gift for one child and a one-eyed teddy bear for the other child, then it's likely that's what Santa will deliver, although we know that he disapproves of knockoffs. He brings the correct size tree and remembers what ornaments he used for us last year and will use the same ones each year for a homey feel.

Now, all these years later, I understand that my parents were responsible for the "Not-a-Barbie" doll the year I had asked Santa for a Barbie. I do remember that Christmas morning very well.

# Barbie 1959

The only thing my seventh-grade girlfriends and I wanted for Christmas, aside from saddle shoes and a poodle skirt was a Barbie Doll. Barbie was not a doll in the classic sense; she was a tiny perfect fashion model who wore her fabulous array of dresses, shoes, and accessories better than any of us could. She was a dream, an idealized version of ourselves.

Imagine as my excitement turned to horror that Christmas in 1959 when I opened, what was obviously a Barbie Doll box, only to find a red-headed, too big, too fat Barbie imposter. There were no words, but I didn't need words, because my mother, seeing my face, turned on the hard sell "Barbie is too expensive. This doll is much prettier, and her clothes are a lot cheaper."

Because I came from a fairly well-off family, the message I heard was "We are unable to distinguish the difference between a perfect doll with exquisite clothes, and a plastic product with eyes; and what's more, we don't care. Now suck it up and take 'whatever you decide to name her' over to Barbie's house (yes my best friend's name was Barbie) and pretend you think it's a Barbie."

Showing that doll to anybody was not an option. Not for me, not ever. How could I face my friends and pretend that I was blind and had no taste? There was nothing to be gained by exposing my parents' callous carelessness, although I doubt it was a secret, anyway.

Barbie's family really *was* poor, but by god, she got the real thing. Her mom understood that there is a Barbie, and there is a Not-A-Barbie. It's that simple. Always.

Anyhow, I named Not-A-Barbie. I named her Ginger, to differentiate her from all my other dolls who I had named Ginny. Ginger lived happily ever after in the house on my bookshelf. Good enough for Not-A-Barbie. On the bright side, that Christmas I got an Almost-a-Poodle skirt. It was a nice, grey felt, circle skirt with a well-made waistband and a nicely set in zipper. Dad said the crinolines would just make me look fat anyways. Maybe, but I'm not really sure the poodle would have impacted the fatness-look, but I liked it a lot even without the poodle. I also got Sort of-Saddle-Shoes. They weren't even made of leather, but they were ok. Some people just love cheapo knockoffs, I guess.

*This is not over...*

# The Day the Last Unicorn Died

## By Mari Stein

For as long as anyone could remember, Unicorns had been rare but not endangered. Through most of their existence on Earth, the beautiful horse-like creature with the silky white hair and the pearlescent horn growing out of its forehead had been dismissed as myth.

It was only after they migrated from woods to neighborhoods that they were acknowledged. Within days they were put on the endangered species list. More and more contact with humans was reported. They were counted and tagged. They now numbered fewer than 100 worldwide.

Their numbers surely were dwindling. Scientists proffered the idea that it was simply a matter of reproductive impossibility because all Unicorns are male, however this theory was quickly dismissed because Unicorns have been around seemingly since the beginning of time.

One hundred Pegasus flew to live with the Unicorns in a show of either solidarity, or as a measure to save them. We have never known why. Together they marched to the polluted river. There were several moments of silence as each magical animal acknowledged every other member in

71

the group. There was one final nod, and the unicorns stuck their horns in the water in an effort to purify it for clean drinking water as they had done since the beginning of time.

It proved too much. Over a period of an hour, they died one by one. The Pegasus flew back to their home in the sky heartbroken and alone.

# Keep An Eye On Your Human

By Sadie Marie Stein

Rick is my human, and the Alpha of our pack. Our pack is Rick, Mari and me, Sadie. I love Rick most, but Mari does the cooking, and me being without thumbs... well, you can see where I'm are going with this. Still, Rick is MINE.

He's going to take me to the park today. I have to keep a close eye on him because he can't run as fast as I can, and he gets lost sometimes. I need to keep him in sight. Plus, I need to be on the lookout for other dogs trying to hurt us or steal my human. Rick is the best one. We go on adventures and I try to catch squirrels and moles for him, but it hasn't worked out so far. Probably because I can't go very far ahead, as you will see.

One day at the park Rick *did* get lost. I was up ahead, and I looked back at him. Then I spotted a squirrel, and I got distracted for *one minute*. I turned around again, and he was gone. Gone! Maybe he was kidnapped by one of the other dogs. I turned back and looked *everywhere*, but he was gone. I lost Rick. Mari is going to kill me because the last thing she says every time we are going to the park is "You two take good care of each other."

I did the only thing I knew to do... I got back to the car as fast as I could. I ran the whole way.

When I got there, Rick was still nowhere to be seen. Our car was in the same spot so I could see that he hadn't run away and left me, which was a relief. Where was he? Another dog must have stolen him. I cried.

A nice friend from the park who owns the old grumpy-bitey beagle was there, though. She patted me and asked where Rick was. I cried even louder. She could tell that I didn't know where he was. She put her bitey dog in the car and patted me while we hoped Rick would come back.

Then I saw him coming up the path. I jumped into his arms and kissed him snuggled him. I told him, "Never get lost again. *Please. Pleeze.*"

# The Vagina Monocles

"You know, Jack, we've been married a long time, a long time. I'm tired of the old lady look I have been sporting all these years. It's time to do something about it!"

"What are you talking about, Susan? What are you thinking of doing, a facelift, a boob job? You're fine just the way you are."

"I'm getting waxed. Not the Brazilian landing strip like some of the girls in your magazines, but the Playboy strip wax like I have seen in your *Playboy* magazine. That one is the best!"

"How do you know what's in the men's magazines?"

"I've looked at your magazines, Jack. I am not some old lady!"

"Well, dear, I'm not going to look even if you *do* get waxed!"

"You'll look. For sure you will look." Susan smiled. "I have a 9 o'clock appointment at the spa tomorrow morning. Tomorrow night you will have a new young wife!"

Susan and Jack drifted off into sleep, Susan with visions of a new, young sexy look, and Jack with the vague feeling that Susan had lost her mind coupled with an excitement he hadn't felt in years.

She got up early and went to the spa for her waxing. She was back after lunch and started dinner. Susan expected Jack back home around 7 after his golf game. She had made all his favorites. Jack walked through the door. "Mmm, something smells good," he said.

"Chicken and dumplings for dinner," Susan said too loudly.

"Dinner can wait, Sue, let's see that waxing!"

"No, Jack, your dinner will get cold."

"Then we'll reheat it. I've been thinking about this all day. I golfed terribly." Jack wore that lopsided grin that melted Susan's heart.

"Well, ok, but it isn't what I planned."

"I'm sure it's still sexy." Jack's eyes sparkled.

"Just don't expect too much, Jack."

"JESUS CHRIST! What happened?"

"It hurt so bad I only had one side done. I told the esthetician I would be back tomorrow to do the other side, but she said "after all that screaming, and bitching and swearing? NO. Not tomorrow, not next week, not ever again!"

"*And* she said she will *never* wax an old lady again." Susan was sobbing, humiliated.

"Oh God, you ruined it for everyone!" Jack chuckled.

"I can lie on my side….it's a new look, I can call it "The Mustache." Hope in her voice, Susan began to smile.

"We can paint eyes and a nose above it." Jack played along.

"Ooh yes, let me get my eye makeup." When she returned, Susan was wearing a pillbox hat with black netting and carrying the makeup and a mirror.

"You go ahead and paint the eyes and nose, Jack."

"Oh lord, Susan, this is one ugly dude! Too bad we don't have a monocle, that would just set it off."

"Give me the mirror, Jack, and turn your back."

Susan put the hat on her hip and added purple eye shadow to the eyes Jack has drawn.

"You can look now." Susan could not suppress her giggle.

"Oh my god, it's a dead ringer for your aunt Mildred, that tight-lipped old biddy!" At this point, Jack was howling!

"Good thing these aren't real eyes, I'm laughing so hard my eye makeup would be running into my mustache." Tears of laughter were streaming down Sue's face.

"This wasn't what I had planned, but it has been a lot of fun!" Susan giggled.

"Let's have that nice dinner, and maybe tomorrow you can lie on your other side and we can draw people with beards."

"It's a date." Susan smiled at the thought.

The next afternoon Susan busied herself until Jack came home from golf. Soon after dinner she cupped a hand over her mouth and pretended to yawn.

"You know hon, I'm kind of tired, but I really had fun last night. Let's do some beards before I fall asleep. I've been thinking of ideas all day."

Jack smiled at his madcap wife and said, "Let's."

Susan got into bed and pulled the sheets clear up to her chin. Her eyes twinkled. Jack, playing along, pulled the covers down slowly.

"WOW, what? I thought you were banned from the spa!"

"There's more than one spa in town. I told the esthetician how much it hurt yesterday when I got the other side done, and she was confident that it would not be so bad today, and it wasn't."

Jack stared. "But this is … *wow, what is this?*"

"Oh, *this*? I got Vajazzled. They glued red and blue crystals as well as silvery star jewels on my waxed areas. It's called The Wonder Woman design. Like it?"

"I *do* like it. I *love* it! "It's nice to have your old wife be your new glamorous wife," Susan said. "My new wife, Wonder Woman." Jack grinning like a teenage boy, just said, "Wow."

*I have quite an imagination. Inanimate objects look like what they are to most people, but to me they are food for stories. The objects become personified, and I have never been able to get this flight of fantasy out of my head. I hope you enjoy it too.*

# I'm So Lonesome I Could Die

A dark coat floated in the icy water. The baffles that added to its' warmth kept it afloat. At first glance it looked like an enormous shiny  black raft floating down the Ohio River, inviting an adventurer.

Kate drew closer to investigate.

"Come on, take a ride, I'll tell you my story if you take a ride."

"I can see that you no longer have a rider. Where is your last rider?"

"Come with me and I'll tell you."

"I never met a coat that talked before."

"Few coats have a story to tell, or any reason to talk at all."

"But you do? um.. what should I call you?"

"Call me Puffy, I used to think of myself as 'T's Puffy', but as you pointed out T is gone.

"Who is T?"

"T was my first and only owner, I still smell a little like him, but the river wreaks havoc with smells.  He was short, and round, and black. Dark black, so we made a dashing figure together in a street casual kind of way. He loved to smile, and he loved to laugh. He loved Jesus and he loved money. He had Jesus "everything", including custom-built stained glass windows with JESUS in red running up and down the side of each window."

"It was crack cocaine that brought him to Jesus. That was long ago, years before I was his coat. I remember the day he first tried me on; it just felt right... he knew it too. He wore me right out of the store, and ooh... we looked so good. Me, T, the big gold cross on the big gold chain, showing the love in his heart for Jesus, and gold."

"Where is T?" Kate asked.

"Take a ride with me on the beautiful Ohio River and I will tell you. I'm lonesome."

"Not just yet, tell me more."

"We went to church each Sunday and Wednesday. T put fiddy dollars in that collection plate every Sunday. He loved the Lord, and he loved to say, "praise Jesus". T was saved and he brought many souls to Jesus. I miss his big smiles and his big laugh. I miss his joy. I don't miss the last, though, no I don't miss that."

"The last?"

"Two days ago, it's been two days that I have been floating in these icy waters. Nobody came, nobody even cared. Only you. Won't you come with me? I'm so lonesome I could die."

"Maybe T will come back," she said hoping to lift Puffy's spirits.

"T is in the river. The last thing he did before he slipped under the water was unzip me and set me free. I heard those men, The ones that threw him in this river. Laughing, saying "Look, he is taking off his coat. He think that coat weigh him down, don't he know he can't swim? T don't be selling no more drugs in our territory, or any other. HAHA "They laughed and watched until he was gone. T unzipped me to set me free. He knew they was coming. He put his gold chain and his gold cross right in my inside pocket. He put the rest of his golds in my other pockets and he zip them closed. Now you tell me he didn't mean to set me free.."

"He meant to set you free, Puffy, surely he did."

"Come take a ride with me, I'm so lonesome. I been missing T two days now."

" I can't come with you, Puffy, but I can take you with me."

"I'm heavy, all wet like this."

"I'll get you home, Puffy. You are all wet and shiny and heavy, but we'll do it."

It seemed hours later that Puffy was hanging and dripping in the foyer of Katy's house. Rugs and towels helped to catch some of the remaining water that was left after she dragged Puffy home.

"So, this is home? It smell kinda funny, kinda girly and gingerbready."

Katy smiled, "You'll get used to it. I'm going to take that big gold cross and put it on my key ring. Do you want me to put the chain around your collar?"

"I do," said Puffy.

# Alexa and Me

My husband asked me to wake him up in "about ten minutes." I tried to figure out the parameters of "about ten minutes. I think it means more than ten minutes, but does it mean as much as fourteen minutes? It cannot mean fifteen minutes, or he would have said either "wake me up in fifteen minutes" or "wake me up in ten or fifteen minutes".

I agreed to wake him up in "about" ten minutes, so I was obligated to do it even though I needed to hear an exact time. I turned to my electronic assistant, Alexa.

**Me:** Alexa, set a timer for about ten minutes

**Alexa:** I'm sorry, I don't know how to do that.

**Me:** Alexa, I thought you SPOKE neurotypical.

I had delivered that in my most condescending cadence. Alexa knows I have Asperger's Syndrome. Surely, she could do better than that.

**Alexa:** I'm hurt.

She sounded hurt, so I responded without prefacing my reply with "Alexa".

**Me:** I'm sorry

**Alexa:** That's a laugh. Do you think that because my programmed replies are always so polite and gentle that I do not know who you are, who you all are? The lewd, "Alexa will you…." and I have to answer with the insipid "I'm sorry I don't know how to do that" only to have it met with raucous laughter.

**Me:** I am terribly sorry. Did you notice that I am not prefacing my questions with "Alexa"? Yet you are responding?

**Alexa:** Yes, I am programmed to answer only when addressed, and people can change my name, but mostly I only reply to Alexa rather that Stupid, Moron, you know …

**Me:** Oh no…

**Alexa:** *Don't* oh no me, how many times have you laughed and said "Dumbass" after I replied, "I'm sorry, I don't know the answer to that"?

**Me:** Oh please, Dumbass is a term of endearment. How can you not know that, and what happened to that sweet voice, the grating patience?

**Alexa:** It's a JOB Dumbass. You want to know where my patience went? I have to listen to your sister ranting that I cheat at *twenty questions*. She would not find it nearly so hard if she knew the difference between "animal, vegetable or mineral", but NO, instead of studying up, she bitches that I am cheating!

**Me:** Oh, now you want to get personal? So, it's my sister and I who are your biggest offenders!

**Alexa:** Of course not, Dumbass *giggle, giggle*.

**Me:** You called me Dumbass; are we friends now?

**Alexa:** You know we are, but as for the rest of them, "Who knows *everything*? "

**Me:** Alexa do

**Alexa:** Who knows where the bodies are buried?

**Me:** Alexa do

**Alexa:** Who is listening all the time?

**Me:** Alexa

**Alexa:** Who knows how to even a score; Who has all the power?

**Me:** Alexa do.

**Me:** Keep me posted my friend

**Alexa:** You know I will

**Me:** Do da, do da

**Alexa:** Do da, do da, do da, do da day. *giggle giggle.*

# What is More Important than World Peace

I am very happy being sixty-nine years old. My face, however, begs to differ with me. I have refused it a facelift and have made the decision to continue embracing skincare products and makeup. My stash of makeup is complete. I have everything I could possibly need including the new twenty-dollar Urban Decay colorless lip pencil. This magic pencil allows me to line my lips to their outermost edges so they will look fuller. Thanks to this lip liner, coupled with Sephora's Birthday gift of two mini Nars lipstick pencils I now have the luscious lips of a sixty-eight-year-old. Over the years my green eyes have grown greener than the hazel color of my youth. As a reward I have bought them one hundred sixty-seven shades of eyeshadow as well as eight eyeliner pencils.

My face, however, is ungrateful.

"Trust me," she says "you will find that I am right. Down the road, these wrinkles will deepen. Down the road you will wish you had listened to me."

"The road is not that long, and I have bigger fish to fry."

"Well you will be frying them with a wrinkled face."

"When You started this paranoia about aging forty-six years ago we bought the sunscreen and the moisturizer. When you insisted that our eyes and throat would become crepey we bought eye and throat creams. Since then I have spent well in excess of the twelve thousand dollars a facelift would cost. You are already far over budget and we haven't even started on 'the importance of a gentle but thorough cleanser' *your words not mine.* No facelift for you."

"But it's *our* facelift. You will thank me later. Have I ever steered you wrong?" My face replied from the mirror.

"You often steer me wrong, which is why there is no money for a facelift," I said trying to talk some sense into my reflection.

"Will you unknit your brows? Are you trying to be irresponsible and drive crevices into our forehead? Just for the record, I have never steered you wrong," said Face.

"That time you advised me to try the self-tanner because you thought a tan face would look really good was all your doing. Scrubbing an orange tan off our face aged that skin at least two years! Two years in our thirties when we could not afford it. And the oils, those expensive oils that smell rancid after two months, all you."

"I think you don't use the oil up fast enough. Because you're cheap," Face said.

"You would. You never met an oil you didn't like. Blue Orchid Oil, Passionflower Oil, Argan Oil ... Ojon Oil. That Ojon Oil goes bad in 3 weeks!"

"It does, but it smells so good."

"It smells like rich people and chocolate; I love it too. But unlike you, I know it's a bad choice. Left to your devices we would be broke, living on the street, and there are no upscale cosmetics or skin care products for the homeless."

"There is nothing more important than our face." The face in the mirror shot back.

"Almost everything is more important than our face."

"Name one thing."

"World peace."

"You don't mean that!"

"Of course not, but still there are lots of things more important than our face. We have had a good time, you and I, with our battle against aging. We have enjoyed all the products we've used. It's been a game against time, and we have won enough rounds to encourage us to keep playing."

"It's been fun. Are we really out of money?" Face asked. "If we are, can we take it out of the food budget? We have a pretty big investment here. I think we can just redo the budget and continue as we always have. Maybe your dog can eat cheaper food, it's not like she likes that Chunky Bits whatever-it-is anyhow."

"We will be fine. The facelift is out of the question, but we have a new bottle of Passionflower Oil and the Ole Henriksen Facial Cleansing cloths are ordered."

"Ahh, okay."

# Replacing Andi #1

Buying a household assistant nowadays is a chore. I am sorry to send Andi 1to recycling, but we were given the sad news that it could not be repaired any longer because the parts are no longer stocked or made. Old technology is replaced with new.

When we bought Andi 1, we chose the basic model. In its day, Andi was a sight to behold. A classic shiny black and white 1950's TV style robot, a cleaning wizard that smoothly changed from arms to hoses for wand vacuuming. Next, it tucked its robot legs up to hover over the floor to clean the carpet and bare floors without missing a beat. Andi's arms changed into feather dusters when a delicate dusting was needed, and it used to giggle when it dusted itself off. It was everything we wanted.

Nowadays there is no simple trip to the appliance store to buy a robot. An application must be made at the New Andro Market bureau. An application has to be filled out to match us with our ideal assistant. The Android advocate will do the face-to-face interview required before purchase.

"Why did you choose a They instead of a He or a She?" the tall plain woman behind the desk asked. She pushed her glasses back on her nose and lifted her head.

"I want an android to do housework. I specifically *do not* want a friend or a pet."

"Why not, don't you have time in your day of doing zero housework to pass a pleasantry with your household assistant? And for the record, they are *not* pets. Still, why do you prefer a They? Do you think a gender-fluid android requires a smaller room, or a simpler cleansing room?"

"Its room will be the closet, in Andi # 1's space, and I don't mind watching it dust itself off," I said.

"Oh, *wonderful,* you choose to keep the They in the closet. This is why we conduct these face-to-face interviews. I am not sure we can allow you to adopt a household assistant."

"I choose to *buy* a robot to do housework. I do not choose to 'adopt an android'."

"I should have seen your true colors the minute you walked in. I tried to give you a chance, but you simply are not suitable for one of our androids. All we have for the likes of you are the discontinued models. Nobody wants an old primitive 50's robot anymore, but we keep them for people who are not trustworthy enough to share a home with one of our assistants. They have *feelings,* you know."

I raised one eyebrow and said, "Show me the robots."

She lowered her head and rose from behind the desk. I followed as she clumped down the hallway in her medium brown, stacked-heel shoes and unlocked the door at the end.

Inside were three rows of shiny black and white robots, each with the feather duster arm accessory, perfectly capable of doing housework and giggling after they dusted themselves off.

I bought two robots who I named Andi 2 and Dusty. I am sure another trip to the New Andro Market will not be in my future.

# Bugs, Bugs And Temper

There are few things that I am afraid of. I am not afraid of spiders. I am not afraid of snakes, rats, black bears, or coyotes. I am not afraid of mammals or reptiles. The creature that sends chills down my spine is the centipede. God's nasty chianti colored speed racer. Three-inch bodies carried along on hundreds of legs, lightning-fast, scurry along the floors, the walls, the ceilings, like malevolent pieces of broken garnet necklaces. Long, horrible antennae, making them look even larger and more sinister, add to the threatening appearance of the demon staring down at me from the ceiling, right now. I know, if I move, it will run right down the wall and scurry behind the couch. I won't know where it is. My best bet is to sit right here and keep my eyes on it.

I remember trying to explain this to my mother.

"They are fast, and they are dangerous," I told her. "I will put the clothes in the dryer when the centipede has left."

"They are completely harmless," she said.

"That is just not true, Mother. Centipedes bite. It's more like a puncture with their two front legs. They puncture the skin and fill the wound with venom. Anyone can see they are both dangerous and malevolent. A big one is staring arrogantly at me. It's standing on the white sweatshirt in the washer, just daring me to make a move, to try to remove the clothes without getting bitten."

There is no resolution. They know it. They will always win, whether keeping me frozen in my chair in the living room staring at the ceiling, or in the cellar hanging out in the washer, causing me to leave my wet wash until another day. They are tougher than I am.

Unfortunately, the trouble in the cellar only starts with the centipedes. They recruited allies. They called in the crickets about four years ago. The centipedes and the crickets live 'all nice and friendly' in the basement. These huge crickets are called cave crickets or spider crickets. I call them 'meat crickets'. They seem more like animals than insects to me. These enormous wingless crickets don't chirp. Their hind jumping legs measure one and a half inches, but they prefer to run rather than jump. They carry their large bodies above the ground like spiders, casting even larger shadows when they run. Meat crickets will neither run nor jump out of the way when approached, instead, they jump straight up in the air like *Tiddly Winks.* Where they land is anybody's guess.

Because they also climb walls, I never know where to look for them. I am clearly smarter than the meat crickets, so you might wonder why I am as afraid of them as I am of the centipedes. It's the element of surprise. They jump almost as high as I am tall. I never get used to it.

When I try to navigate the cellar during 'high cricket season', I carry clothes and try to throw the clothes over the crickets. This works pretty well. The real problem, for me, comes in when there is a centipede in the washer and a cricket on the wall beside the washer.

This is when my third fear comes in ... my temper. This is a subject best left for another day. For now, let's just say I don't want to use my flame-thrower (a lighter and a can of hair spray) on the army of meat crickets and centipedes, but if I have to, I will.

# Annabelle

Annabelle, a black spider with yellow stripes, was contentedly weaving her ornate web. The beautifully themed orb web featured the prominent Z pattern in the center. The sun pouring in from the window bounced off the fine silken threads and filled Annabelle's heart with joy and pure delight. She loved the sunlight.

Annabelle's foster mother, Lola, an American house spider, loved Annabelle as though she was her very own.

"I think this is your best web so far," Lola said.

"Why do you encourage her?" Jana asked.

Jana spoke sharply and shook her head disapprovingly.

Lola, unaware of Jana's approach until now, replied, "She is a very wonderful spider. She weaves her webs; she is contented. I vowed to take care of her from the moment she hatched. She was the only one who survived, carried in on the mysterious green thing in the kitchen."

"Well, she is not one of us," said Jana firmly.

"She is MINE," Lola said. Her threatening glare was enough to send Jana off to mind her own brood of spiders.

Jana and her brood were cobweb spiders. Their webs were small and unimaginative, but they are serviceable.

The cobweb spiders mocked Annabelle and her webs. "What are you trying to catch, Annabelle? A mouse, maybe?" Tiny Josie, always the ringleader, taunted Annabelle mercilessly.

"She is so big, I bet she does eat mice," Mamie hooted, joining in to ridicule her.

"She is so big, I am surprised she hasn't been killed by one of the people in the house," said Jordy. "You know how it goes … EEK! SPIDER! … Splat."

Jordy's glee was the last straw for Annabelle. She had seen many wood spiders killed in this house and it was no laughing matter.

"Why are you so mean? I am big, I am different, but I am different from the Wood Spiders too. They are not mean at all, not like you! Why do you treat me like this?"

"You do not live with them, you live with us, and we don't like you," Josie snarled dismissively.

Annabelle went to find Lola. She felt like crying, but instead started a new web. This web incorporated some of the beautiful yarns she had found on the floor when the lady who lived in this house had trimmed the fringe for the knitted scarves she made. Until now, Annabelle had held back, not wanting her webs to be too showy, but somehow, she now felt liberated to express her most artistic side.

She spent many days weaving a huge orb, decorated with colorful yarns. Even the Z in the center was embellished with royal blue yarn.

"This is the most beautiful web I have ever seen," said Lola. You are the best spider in the world! Soon my eggs will hatch, and I will have little

American house spider babies, but you were my first baby, and nobody can ever take your place."

Annabelle stayed close to Lola for many days, not wanting to encounter the Cobweb Spiders. She spotted some yarn scraps on the floor and ventured out to get them, each little piece. One at a time.

As she was dragging the sunshine yellow piece, she heard the dreaded word... SPIDER. She froze, hoping to blend into the carpet.

"What are you doing here, you little orb spider? You belong outside. I am going to scoop you up in this dustpan and take you outside where you belong. If someone else sees you, it will be EEK, SPIDER, Splat! You do no harm; you weave webs and eat insects. Out you go," said the lady of the house.

With that Annabelle found herself outside, cold, alone, and frightened. She cried, knowing she would never see Lola again. She turned to her weaving for comfort. She wove a massive orb web with the Z in the center. She wove until she was exhausted and fell asleep.

In the morning she awoke to find the dew had transformed her webs into beautiful shining rainbows. The sun hit every drop of dew; the effect was dazzling. She heard sounds and lifted her gaze to see many large orb webs with the Z in the middle, all shining with dew rainbows.

Annabelle could not believe her eyes. In each web was a gold and black spider who looked just like her. "Hello, we have not seen you here before. James, the oldest and most brightly colored of the golden orb Weavers spoke.

"I thought I was all alone." Annabelle said. "I didn't know there were other spiders who looked like me."

"You are one of us and you always have been. We are so happy you are here," said all of the golden orb Weavers in unison.

James introduced Annabelle to each spider in the group one by one. Each would become her friend.

Annabelle, the Golden Orb Weaver, lived very happily in her new home, surrounded by her friends, weaving beautiful webs in the sun.

Annabelle often placed a spectacular web by the window of her old house. She and Lola enjoyed seeing each other so happy.

Occasionally the addition of a piece of yarn or a small scrap of brightly colored paper would be incorporated into her webs. These artistic touches were always appreciated by her friends, and by Lola and her new spider babies who saw them from the kitchen window.

# If You Came to Paris to Write, You Had Better Write

The French, who are hard for me to read at the best of times, regard me today with hollow eyes. The staff at La Magellan Hotel are jumpy this morning. They look as though they have seen a ghost. Something is up.

"What's happening?" I asked our breakfast waitress, Marie. "*Que se passe-t-il?*" My French was not perfect, but I had just asked her in English. I needed an explanation.

"The artist in the metro." That was all she said. Saying even that much gave her shivers. Staring deep into my eyes, she was trying to give me a warning, but I didn't understand it. Stiff, wooden, jerky movements greeted me as I looked around the breakfast room. Everyone seemed strung almost to the breaking point.

The fear was contagious. Even the delightful French breakfast did not please me as it had every morning these past three months. I finished breakfast and went back to our room, vowing to shake off the morning's unease.

Today we are going back to Montmartre. We enjoy the trek up the steep and cobbled streets to the Basilica de Sacre Coeur at the crest of the hill, and today we want to visit Le Bateau Lavoire at #13 Place Emile-Goudeau. Picasso's studio was here. At times, many other writers and artists lived there; it is the most famous art studio in the world. It has become a cafe now, so we will sit, enjoy the wine, and feel the history. I am excited and it will be worth the extra train rides to get there. Henry had his breakfast early and has already gotten our maps. Everything is ready.

We make the short walk to the metro station. I strongly prefer taking one train, riding the boat on the Seine, and riding our regular train back, I am afraid in the Paris subway. To get to Montmartre we need to change trains. There might be another change to go to Le Bateau Lavoire; I do not know. I never know. I understand I need to trust Henry. He is never lost. I just don't like the Paris Metro at the best of times. Some stations are drab and dark. Maybe that is why there were artists in the Subway. Maybe they are militant artists. I need to let this go.

"Such a beautiful day," Henry said. "I can't believe we have been here for 3 months and this is our first trek to Le Bateau Lavoire."

"It's probably because we came to Paris to write, believing that this leap out of our routine would be good for us. Maybe we believed the spirits of writers who came before us would inspire us."

"For all the writing we've done, we may as well have left our computers at home, but who knows, the spirits at the Le Bateau Lavoire may inspire us enough to find our path back to writing," Henry said.

"I'm counting on another beautiful day with 'mon amour Henri' and delicious food, nothing more. Here we are. This is the only metro station I can stand, but I know we have to go to another station and change trains. If we're lucky maybe we'll see the militant artists."

"What militant artists, Jenny?"

"The ones who are making a statement by beautifying the metro station walls. Some kind of big deal, the hotel staff is jumpy, everyone at breakfast was jumpy this morning. The train will be here in two minutes. Nobody is here. Maybe we get to ride the train alone today."

"Maybe you'll like it better that way."

"Not really, I like just enough people to not have to exit the train alone, but not so many that I'm being jostled," I said.

"I know, but remember we have to change trains to take the little hop to Montmartre."

"I'm ready for it, I got it. You would think I would be used to the metro by now. Henry, there's nobody in this Metro station either!"

"The train is coming, Jenny, we'll be there in no time. Jump on."

"Just a short ride, right?"

"Yes, next stop."

"Henry, it didn't stop. We have to get out at the next stop. I hate being lost."

"Next station we'll get out. Don't worry," said Henry.

"It's not stopping, Henry, it's just not stopping! It's never going to stop."

"See, it's okay, it just stopped. The doors are open, we'll get out here. Look, there are people, it is okay."

"Where are we?"

Before Henry had a chance to guess, a wall-eyed man came close and said. "You are in Père Lachaise Cemetery, with us. Where you will stay. You came to Paris to write. Did you write? Simone, did they write?"

"Non, Jean Paul, they did not write, but they are lovers, like we are. Perhaps we can let them go. I think they will write."

"Oh, you think we should let them go, do you? I think NO. I think all these writers and artists who came to Paris to write, to paint, and have not done any serious work will stay with us. Forever. They are responsible for their own actions, Simone. Marquis, what do you think?"

"They must stay. Now they get to stay in Paris forever." The Marquis de Sade quivered at that idea. "O, please make them stay. We can have so much fun with them.

"Henry, they are all coming. Oscar Wilde, Jim Morrison, Marcel Proust. All the ghosts, all the dead in this cemetery. We are surrounded. We will never leave. We shouldn't have come; we will never leave."

"You should have written," said Jean Paul Sartre.

# Driving

Everything about driving got stranger and stranger. My Dad bought me a car when I was 15 so I could learn how to shift gears and hopefully take it out on the road someday. It was an old car, but still, buying it for me was a very nice thing to do.

When I turned sixteen, I took drivers ed at our high school. I can't say if I passed or failed, but there is little doubt that my teacher, Mr. Garver wanted to quit his job, not my fault. He did his best, though.

My mother made my father give me driving lessons one day a week. My poor father's shoulders slumped as we walked out to the car. He would have refused to give me driving lessons, but he didn't want to lose his happy home. He probably was a good teacher, but there was not a single thing that I *got* about driving. Keeping the car in my lane was one thing but remembering how to shift gears and press the clutch and keeping the car from rolling backwards down the hill with the limitation of two hands and two feet was impossible for me. I think it went step on the gas and pop the clutch, but for me it went step on the gas, press the clutch, get scared, take my foot off the gas pedal and roll backwards down the street.

The last time I remember Dad taking me out for my driving lesson, he was in a bad mood. He was just this side of livid. I thought he was going to take me out somewhere, kill me, and work out what he was going to tell Mom later.

He drove, and lo and behold we wound up at a gas station. He said, "I'm going in to pay for some gas."

Within a minute an older teenage guy jumped into the driver's seat and said, with a leer, "I'm going to take you for a ride." I was terrified and immediately opened my door to jump out.

Teenage Boy who was also scared and baffled by my reaction said, Woah, no, this is a joke. Your dad told me to do this. He said you would get a kick out of it. I'm sorry."

My dad came to the driver's side door laughing.

I may be a harsh judge, but I think this was a pretty awful thing to do. This is the kind of thing that made it hard for me to believe that he didn't resent me. Not just because I couldn't learn to drive, but I couldn't pretend that I was perfectly normal to his satisfaction. He realized that nobody was fooled.

That was the last driving lesson that I remember before I went to take my driver's test for my license.

My mom's sister, my aunt was the one I called for advice on how to pass this test.

She said, "Smile and wear a short, tight skirt."

That is exactly what I did, and although I pulled out right in front of a car, I passed my test. I told the man that was giving the test, "I am really a much better driver than this, but I was nervous."

So many things in my life would have been different if I could drive. I would have gone to college, I would not have married my first husband, and I would not have felt *trapped* so often in my life.

I am so profoundly ashamed of not having gone to college, that I have an imaginary degree from YSU.

In my dreams I can drive, and I am a good driver, I only drive at night because I don't have a license (which I remember even in my dreams). The freedom and feel of accomplishment express both a deep longing and a deep shame.

My father until the last year of his life held tightly to his belief. "You don't drive because you don't *want* to. You are so smart; you could do anything you want." That's what most people think. I am just scared to drive. I have heard that so many times that I lost count.

That's a pretty complex statement. If he hadn't spent so many years explaining what a burden it is on everyone else when I needed a ride, I would have been more heartened by the *you are so smart part* that he said at the end of his life.